The Early Hours

Collected Poems

2013-2021

Adam Gary

www.adamgary.co.uk

Instagram: @adamgary

YouTube: Adam Gary Poetry

Cover Art by
Sophie Scarlette
@sentientstardustpoetry
www.philosophieblog.wixsite.com/sophiescarlette

Cover Design by author.

Dedication: to everything I lost in the last 2 years.
to everything I gained.

Other works by the author:

Poetry:
Poetry in Motion

-

White Cover Trilogy:
The Random Ramblings of a Restless Mind
Blue Streak
Poet in the Long Dark Coat

-

The Early Hours

Fiction:
Southwest on the A303

Contents

Contents

INTRODUCTION

It has certainly been a while since I have written an introduction to a new poetry collection. *The Early Hours* came about having spent the last two years working on my YouTube channel, doing everything I can to help new poets who, like me, find themselves enthralled by the craft but don't necessarily have the know how to better themselves. I was never an academic and often bunked poetry classes in school. Irony. I try to be the teacher I needed back then.

During this time on YouTube I have reviewed contemporary's self-published collections and been wowed by them, as well as some traditionally published collections that completely let me down. I knew I had to set an example to some, and up my game to others. I have also seen first hand just how insecure we can be as poets often receiving messages from my followers about how they don't feel good enough. This is my way of leading by example.

I have learnt so much the past few years about poetry, what it means to write it, and the journey it takes to go from a beginner to a novice (I believe this journey I'm on is going to be a neverending one of discovery and am by no means a 'Master'). And so to cut a long story a little shorter, I wanted to show my followers that the journey we're on is something to be proud of. This book contains poems stretching across my entire journey so far. Reading some of the poems from 2013 made me so embarrassed but it was important to me that I felt comfortable with that, and after a little reworking to implement some of my new styles and tastes of 2021, I am happy to be bringing *The Early Hours* to you all.

The titular poem 'The Early Hours' that closes this collection itself speaks and summarises what I have spoken about in the introduction. I hope readers will find comfort in it and realise that this is all a process we have to go through, and that if we pay our dues, if we study hard... anything is possible.

Adam x

The Poet's Role

The poet's role is not to rhyme.
tis not to enjamb or
write lyrically.
Not to capitalise, grammarise
or even spell correctly.
The poet's role is to capture
humanity's soul;
History passed by in a blink
but forever held in the poet's ink.
To rouse, and to sooth.
Romanticise and fantasise.
To love, and smile, and frown and curse and hate.

They may use tools and train
to heighten the words they spake
but that is not
the poet's
role.
Do not
get carried away
but carry away.

(previously uncollected)

A Poem

I sit at my desk
Turning
This beautiful blank page
Into scribbled mess of mundane.

Insane, I am to think that such things
Are of interest to anyone.
That my words, my thoughts,
Are worthy of *any body's* time.

When really all that is at the back of my mind
Is 'when can I put my feet up again and
Grow my belly tenfold(*s*).'

Is a poem really a poem, when it's just random ramblings?
What is a poem?
What is art?

I'm just getting my release and silencing the urges,
But I guess it's a start.

(previously uncollected)

A Poet's Poem

This poem
sucks.
I am just a man amongst many men
amongst many women
amongst many children
amongst many beings,
And I cannot write.
I may write in rhyme and metre
In form and with tools.
But there is still
a silence
over me.
I cannot write.
I cannot write
and it bugs me because I can write.
I cannot write.
This poem sucks and I know it
Heart contrite and contracting ribs
Why
Can I not
Write
When all I can do
is write?

(previously uncollected)

I Think We've Lost It, Mate!

Mindless labyrinth of wild wonder,
Enveloped in stories of unicorn steeds.
Neglect is a dastardly fiend,
Ticking time bomb before an overspilled, invisible plunder.
Arson of the cerebrum
Letting flames spread uncurbed.
Hell dressed as a freedom fighter.
Every eye locked to mock and spy,
"aren't they a little disturbed"…

And from time to time my mind tangles too,
Like long discarded cables and wires,
Thoughtfully getting fantasy and reality completely confused.
'Help' a word I never call,
For I think I'm rather enjoying this fall.
Silence.
No hands reached for mine… or theirs.
Or a comforting arm over the shoulder.
Just rolling eyes
Or chuckles and snarky mutterings
Killing us slowly in our
Fantastical inebriated state,
"Eh, I think we've lost it mate!"

(previously uncollected)

Poetry

Poetry.
The way it bleeds from your heart
Like the soothing compositions of Mozart.
Like the valleys of Avinyar,
And the meadows at Clattinger Farm.

Or perhaps

just a freshly poured pint,
sitting atop an oak finished bar.
Poetry.

Explore, express,
find comfort in your words.
Play arOUnd and be f r e e
Ignore stale rules
And gatekeeping fools.
Think second, write first, stand up and
be   heard.

The joy it brings,
And the beauty it sings,
I'd be lying if I said I wasn't
Hooked.
Poetry.

(originally collected in 'Poetry in Motion' - 2013)

Fern

And oh but her hair be so soft and curled
Like freshly plucked feathers of a Goldfinch
Her eyes alike vast and open worlds
And ones that I explore by ev'ry inch
And her arms wrap around me dearly like
A possum clinging to it's lover
For Cupid's bow did strike with all its might
And sow a seed of love to bloom a wonder
And though they say we are like moths to flame
Diseased with murky infatuation
Tis merely their mindless pungent declaim
Replacing their own dead love's stagnation
But worry not my love, my dear, my muse
If you love me pure, my heart you could never lose

(originally collected in 'Poet in the Long Dark Coat' - 2019)

Micro Poems
Pt. I

A Poet Through The Night

I'm up through the night
If I don't write.
It's like a beast inside of me
Roaring and clawing to get free.
I'm up through the night if I don't write.
My blood thickens and my brain cries,
My hands sweat and my heart dies.
I'm up through the night if I don't write.
My hands jitter and shake,
Which keeps me awake.
I itch and scratch and my mind won't settle
Until I flick on the kettle and reach for my quill.

I'm up through the night
Once I start to write.

(originally collected in 'Blue Streak' - 2018)

Poet's Love

He made love to her so passionately
that gods gathered round in awe,
for a poet's love knows no measure.

(originally collected in 'Blue Streak' - 2018)

Tonight I light a Candle

Tonight I light a candle
For the lovers never found
For the buds that never bloomed.
Tonight I light a candle
For the musicians too scared to play their sound
The audience too shut off and never moved.
Tonight I light a candle
For the glass that cracked
And the leaf first to fall.
For the broken hearted
And the rejected.
There's a lot of hurt in this world
So tonight I light a candle
Yes, tonight I light a candle
And this one's just for you.

(previously uncollected)

On Ageing
(as a panicked 29 year old nobody)

We blink and it's gone.
Hair in every crevice grows,
Our waistbands expand,
Aching bones. Chasing sand but
That's Life. We blink and it's gone.

(previously uncollected)

untittled

it's the simple things
in life that mean the most.

it's been said before a hundred times over,
i know,
but enjoy
the football game, the walk
in the park,
coffee with a friend,
and the butter on toast

because stress in life comes in
abundance, and it's not until
you take notice of
the things we take for
granted that your spirit attains
true ascendance.

(originally collected in 'The Random Ramblings of a Restless
Mind' - 2017)

Writing Desk

Coffee stained oak wood table,
Supporting countless words/
Bring me into existence.

(originally collected in 'Blue Streak' - 2018)

Last Dance

There she sat,
Drinking from a bottle of unmet desire.
Unfulfilled potential and promises.
Smoke clogging her insides
She's an extinguished fire.

And she dialled number after number
Slipping into poisoned slumber,
The world passing her by
Without even a glance.
A curse and a sigh
She missed her last dance
Her heart ever number.

(originally collected in 'Poet in the Long Dark Coat' - 2019)

Knots

And there was something there, something more.
Something which lingered amongst our eyes caught.
Something between those smiles and mindful knots,
Something we wished we had said,
but did not.

(originally collected in 'Blue Streak' - 2018)

Ever Regretful

But I might weep a little longer here
Cradling a blanket of unsought hurt.
For I now stand upon my realised fear
Where darkened cloud reveals a love invert.
That I could slash and leave you bleeding deep
As you lie in bed and cry alone.
Besieged by piked words and feeling cheap
Torturous actions which one must now atone.
But won't you please forgive my hurtful words,
Refill the moulded well.
For trials like these so often will occur
And sands pile in an ever losing race.
So I say that I am so sorry Mum,
Signing yours, your ever regretful Son.

(originally collected in 'Poet in the Long Dark Coat' - 2019)

Bright Eyed

She was once part of the bright eyed happy kind,
Ready to take on the world.
But over time she got left behind,
Battered and bruised by life.

(originally collected in 'Blue Streak' - 2018)

I Tried

I tried to be the person you wanted me to be.
I tried to help set you free.
But understand that by doing that I just couldn't be me.

I couldn't carry you into the southern sea
Baptise you whilst I battle burdens too heavy.
So you see, I had no choice.
And though I love you dearly,
Clearly,
I had to let you go.

So all the best,
And all my love.
Sincerely,

A.G.

(originally collected in 'Blue Streak' - 2018)

What If They Were A...

Fingers never wrapped around my thumb.
Artist's eyes which will never now blink.
They took your heart and left me numb
Having kept me captive 'hind chain-link.

Eros **did** strike mine and mother's heart,
Requiem for a young couple's first love.
Smiling silent and still in Lautrec's bed
Sorrow never seemed so far.

Hours past and turned to weeks
Our silence grew firm from nowhere
Until month three did I finally speak
Learning of her heart's breaking despair
Diploma, adventure, career awaited - she couldn't stall
Her eyes **did** weep a valley, I can promise you this
And I cried 'Alone, I'd do it all', I already loved you after all
Vacant she was, my pleading resist'
Essay prepared of strong will and tough mind
And there was nothing more that I could do
She silenced my heart, and I was resigned
All I wanted was to hold you and to love you
Yet we never got to meet, before they took you away.
Fathers should have a say.

You grow older in mind every single day
And I weep for you every single day
Every single day my torment replayed
Every single day
Every single day

(previously uncollected)

21

A Butterfly In A Snowstorm

She had the beauty of the heavens,
The heart of Orion.
Aphrodite's sensitivity
And the snarl of a lion.
A butterfly in a snowstorm,
A bloomed carnation by a stem of rose.

An unsullied maiden
Left to weep on a bed of woes
For along came a knight of shining black armour.
Ivy to her tower.
Mind and heart grapple in epic
Veronese battle,
For poison did kill the princess
Whom bit the rotten apple.

(previously uncollected)

Flying Fish Of The C

Jumping Jack
Came and went in a flash
Birthed under a raging sun
Another named and characterised
Flying fish of the C

Another blunted shave
With sharpened razor blade
From misinterpretation
Misinformation
Boiling before the simmer
She released one more flying fish
To the turbulent ever populating sea

Sunken ships
Wrecked rowboats with rose
Severed at the spine
Pierced in the heart

Assault or self harm?

Translucent burn scars
Brail on my palm
The story of catching
A flying fish of the C

(previously uncollected)

As I Lay Here

As I lay here with discontented heart
And restless mind once more
In the early hours morn
Belonging to the poets and painters
Philosophers and deep thinkers
The lovers and the loners
My soul cries out for beauty.

Be it from within me
Or out amongst the glimmering stars beyond my window.

I think quietly of my life's problems.
Mistakes and missions.
My life's loves and its undeniable hates.
All I want to do now is write.
My body must rest, but my brain fights.

Tis now the creative hour.
The time our souls leap out from their cages
Of fleshy carcass and sweep up gloriously into the night sky;
Fondly frolicking with one another, creating starry joyful madness
Never to be witnessed by the sleeping mortal.
Oh the elation of such feisty supernatural festivities!
Swirling and swirling, refusing to leave the spectral world
To conjoin with the flesh and bones of their mortal master.

But all too soon sunrise doth come
And whilst the artists finally start drifting off into deep sleep
Unwittingly enjoying their genius' good time
The regular world must shift back into consciousness
To keep the world spinning in its regular routine.

(originally collected in 'The Random Ramblings of a Restless
Mind' - 2017)

Trying To Sleep Through A Night Shift

(but can't stop staring at a Canary Wharf fucking crane light)

Flashing light in the ominous night,
have you come for me? My peripheral
spots you and seldom does she lie.

Be gone flashing light of the ominous night,
who comes again so bold.
Why won't you be told?

Oh, flashing light breaking through the
ominous night,
don't laugh and toy with me
for I'll show you bold!

(originally collected in 'The Random Ramblings of a Restless
Mind' - 2017)

Poetic Quotes
Pt. I

And she stole my heart without even giving me her name.

(originally collected in 'The Random Ramblings of a Restless Mind' - 201

AG

You've inspired every story I've ever written.
You're on every page.
In every line.
You're every word.

(originally collected in 'The Random Ramblings of a Restless Mind' - 2017)

AG

You said you'd always be there,
But when I looked for you in the darkest hour
You were nowhere to be seen.

(originally collected in 'The Random Ramblings of a Restless Mind' - 2017)

And for a brief moment,
we were each other's world.

(originally collected in 'The Random Ramblings of a Restless
Mind' - 2017)

AG

Even in the thickest of mud
you can find a beautiful bloom.

(originally collected in 'The Random Ramblings of a Restless
Mind' - 2017)

AG

Life comes and life goes.
All that matters at the end of it
is whether you've made the right choices
according to your heart.

(originally collected in 'The Random Ramblings of a Restless
Mind' - 2017)

'cos he's just rowing his boat baby,
and you're nothing but his 'ore.

(originally collected in 'Blue Streak' - 2018)

AG

Pain hurts, but at least it's temporary.
Regret… well regret can last forever.

(originally collected in 'Blue Streak' - 2018)

AG

I'm ~~sorry,~~
I'm just not who <u>you</u> wanted me to be.

(originally collected in 'Blue Streak' - 2018)

I can't love whole heartedly
because my heart's not whole

(originally collected in 'Blue Streak' - 2018)

My only regret is not allowing myself to love you sooner.
(originally collected in 'Blue Streak' - 2018)

Her love was lost,
His passion faded.
Life just goes like that I guess.
(originally collected in 'Blue Streak' - 2018)

Keep in mind
That behind every grumpy, stubborn man
Lies a heart unable to mend.

(originally collected in 'The Random Ramblings of a Restless
Mind' - 2017)

s
I'm happy
d

(originally collected in 'The Random Ramblings of a Restless
Mind' - 2017)

All I wanted was for you to
Tell me you loved me,
without saying a word.

(originally collected in 'The Random Ramblings of a Restless
Mind' - 2017)

Poet in the Long Dark Coat

Rain drops were drippin', the clouds swept high,
He stormed out the door if he stayed he would die.
Through soggy marsh fields of dampened green
He popped his collar not wanting to be seen.
Not a word of goodbye, not even a note
So walked the poet in the long dark coat.

Nobody had seen him lurking around
Not even a glimpse, he didn't want to be found.
He was lost in his thoughts as he looked to the sky,
And he wondered if the world was even alive.
Painting pictures with words of his own
Rambled on did the poet in the long dark coat.

He roamed as he pleased from town over town,
Harmonica on mouth playing a sweet sorrowed sound
For he'd seen that the world was all bark and no bite.

And then from afar did he meet her sparkled eye
As she stood in white
Having read the words he'd wrote.
She gave her heart to the poet in the long dark coat.

But it wasn't enough to get him to stay
So she wailed at him and he went on his way.
And was this all that the world would be so willing to show
As they called for the poet in the long dark coat.

And he answered their call without even a thought
For they'd taken the beauty he had so eagerly sought.
They'd already shown him that they just didn't care,
It was all over now, he just wasn't there.
And he raised his gun with a single stroke
So flew did the poet in the long dark coat.

(originally collected in 'Poet in the Long Dark Coat' - 2019)

don't travel public

there's just too much sadness

i was forced to sit on the bus one day
back seat
which smelled of piss and sweat
dribbling manliness
and maybe a hint of downtrodden unhappiness

and i looked around me

there was a thirteen year old mum with her mum
both wearing tracksuits twelve sizes too small
their baby screaming murder
ignored by her flunky mother
there was a bare footed junkie
two future jailbirds in trackies - you know the type
and some poor lonely boy who looked like he wanted to cry
there was a woman who stunk of shit
yelling abuse down the phone
and a lady showing more crack than the crushed pipes
under my foot and seat.

i wondered where the answer lies
but i guess who am *i* to pry.

No.

a cold beer entered my mind and i thought
jesus christ i want to die

(previously uncollected)

book club

let me tell you
being a nice guy certainly has its ~~pricks~~…
perks!

"you're lucky,
i like you," she says
as she places my picture and bio
all
the way down
to
the bottom
where nobody would find me and
my barbaric un-shaven mouth.
hidden conveniently
stored away like an unwanted
moth ridden scarf
forgotten
on the bottom shelf

welcome!

"its a club of powerful womxn
but you're cool so you can join, *i'll let you*, be grateful"
she said
smiling razors
excusing her approving of my participation.
and i smiled nulled murder

if it wasn't for the meat
that flailed between my loins
i thought

id have been welcomed with open arms
giggles, smiles, and dare i say
overzealous embrace
lasting
just a little too long.
i rolled my eyes and sighed
it was a party of
'powerful'
hens
and i
was the only cock at the party

(previously uncollected)

Small Penis'd Leaders

Missiles this way and missiles that way.
We live in a damned world where the leader with the
smallest penis wins.
No brains.
No logic.
Just stupidity and ego.
Time is tick tocking away.
We're here until we're not,
All blown away.

Headlines here, and headlines there. Mass destruction
upon us everywhere. How cruel we are to ourselves, how
we've doomed this race. Though are we surprised? We're
the most destructive race alive!

So needless. So senseless.

Fuck my rhymes!

(originally collected in 'The Random Ramblings of a
Restless Mind' - 2017)

Dingy Dive
Parts I, II, & III

He threw closed his slept in blazer
To keep him from the fierce cold air.
Lifting his collar, fixing his hat and hair.
Igniting a smoke, he passed through Leicester Square
Without a care, ignoring the stares, taking a dirty drag.

Heading through Soho, solo, feeling so low
He made his way for Carnaby Street
Going so slow.
London streets beneath his feet.

He stood on the lamp lit pavement corner and watched the
Street walkers, club promoters and dirty drooling lurkers.
Taking his final drag he flicked the smoke into the road
And continued on his way.

Two lovely ladies headed his way. Locked arms they approached
Smiling.
He tipped his hat as they pushed by, looking him up and down.
Winky wink.

Finally he stood outside 'Ain't nothing but...'
He smiled in front of the lights, winked at the bouncer who knew
him,
And then
He strut in.
He sat in the farthest most corner,
As the sax wailed, veiled by his fedora hat.
Watching as folks frolicked, and bailed.
A cesspool of sweaty hormones, and writhing muscles.
That's the blues.
It gets them going.
He sipped his whiskey and enjoyed the band,
Smiling as the keyboard player trailed.

And as the night grew,
He swayed to and fro
Forgetting he'd felt so low.
Enjoying the curvaceous tight jeans,
And wild thick curls.

He downed his whiskey dregs and walked out his favourite bar
Leaving behind declined lusting blondes, burning loins.
Carnaby Street beneath his feet once more.

He walked over girls drunkenly weeping on the curb
Ignoring the mentally disturbed and drunkenly absurd,
London Baby.
Pathetic swaying brawls between friendly fools
Smiling, amused, for he noticed neither had the bigger balls.
'They're equally shrivelled and small,' he called amusedly.

And before he could end his nightly crawl
The full moon called
Succumbing to the ladies of the night
With ripped fishnet tights and a loving disconnect
Weakening his resolve
Forgetting his haunting regrets.

Taking her for a neat in a Soho dive, down Carnaby Drive
He slapped twenty Adam Smith's on the bar
Just to feel beneath her skirt and bra.
It's a solo night in Soho!
Yolo!

Fighting his extinguished inner glow
Black Raven! Actual Crow.
She asked for more to take it further
But he simply dribbled, 'Sorry love, but I've gotta go.'

(previously collected throughout the White Cover Poetry Trilogy)

A Seagull Stole My Life

A seagull stole my life,
Soaring high with wings wide,
A fucking seagull stole my life.

Sitting hunched over. Back broken from shingle shovelling,
Concrete mixing, aches and pains. Rain.
Destined writer, explorer turned bruise bather … but at least I
have *jazz*.
Sweat on brow, hammer hits slab. Tramontane.
Living between treadmill pillars.
Up and down, and soaring wild. Free from strain.
This seagull acts as a prince of skies,
Living life and stares at me, razzmatazz!
Roaming to and fro, killing me with it's smug
laugh-like gulling.

Soaring high with wings wide
A seagull stole my life.

(previously uncollected)

I'm Too Open

Breathing. Gasping. Feeling.
Grasping the sky with the blink of my eyes,
Bathing in the infinity of being.
Repulsing with the pulsing of life in my veins
They're scared of the honesty.
I'm too open.

Grafting. Sweating. Tasking.
Crafting the tower of heraldry,
Fuelling unapologetically the dual candles.
I'm out of my head.
I'm too open, and that makes them scared.

Mirror of Cogit
Befalls the darkened duvet around them.
Pin pricked peep holes of jealousy
Adjudicating all I've ever known.
I'm too open.

Flying, soaring, unfaltering.
No rope will anchor my kite.
I do as I like, embrace my might,
Forsaken perhaps,
But it's my life.
I'm just too open.

(previously uncollected)

Micro Poems
Pt. II

Sunset on Shere

And as like a bard's blunted quill
With splattered blotched ink
The sun lowered
A red silk blanket
Over our heart shaped box.

(previously uncollected)

The Man With The Volkswagen Camper Van

The man with the Volkswagen camper van.
With his collection of six strings,
And mountain of dusty outdated things,
He's the man with many stories to tell
But remains silent in solitude.
A humble and giving soul
That sticks to good ol' rock n roll.
Teaching me the way of life,
Unwittingly,
Finding beauty in the little things,
The man with the Volkswagen camper van.

(originally collected in 'Poetry in Motion' - 2013)

Clouds

Clouds are cool, aren't they?
In a single moment they are one thing
and then they are able to quickly
become something altogether
quite different. Very adaptable.
I wish I were more like a cloud.

(originally collected in 'The Random Ramblings of a Restless
Mind' - 2017)

Untitled

And there she rolls,
My beautiful English countryside.
My love. My home.
My hills of outstanding natural beauty!
Green trees and gentle breeze.

A romance born
Like something from out of the movies!
And I smile
As she takes me beyond my usual city border,
Hand in hand,
And walks me around Newlands Corner.
Ay, what a wondrous escape to be lost in!

(originally collected in 'Poet in the Long Dark Coat' - 2019)

Man Up, Get A Grip

I was taught to be strong.
To man up and never cry.
Get a grip, get over it,
Real men are tough and never shy.
That to be a man was to be a fortress
With impenetrable walls
We should never let cracks form.
Well, how ironic it is
That those very pressures,
Those exact lies,
Lead to tired eyes from sleepless nights
Worried I would never survive.

(previously uncollected)

Haiku for the 21st Century

Builder ploughs again.
Hammer hits brick, sweat on brow.
So was it worth it?

(originally collected in 'Poet in the Long Dark Coat' - 2019)

I Don't Care

And let the wind blow my hair,
Let the rain drown me down.
Let the mud hug my boots
And the sun burn my skin,
Because life isn't just about being born
And then dying, lying in a grave somewhere.
It's about the fun in getting there!
So blister me,
Dirty me,
Soak me,
Blow me.
I'm just here for the giggles and memories, baby!

(originally collected in 'Poet in the Long Dark Coat' - 2019)

City Lights

City lights, alive at night; damn such a
wonderful sight. Yes.
And after dark, there goes my heart
stolen by your beautiful life.

(originally collected in 'The Random Ramblings of a Restless
Mind' - 2017)

Hurtful Memories

Once upon a time you were my entire reason to breathe
Now nothing more than a familiar stranger
With whom I share hurtful memories

(originally collected in 'Poet in the Long Dark Coat' - 2019)

Sleepless Nights

Do you ever spend sleepless nights in bed
Staring at the space that I one kept
Placing your palm
Replacing my head?

I do.

(previously uncollected)

Once More Unto The Breach

And each time
Someone else's heart is chosen over mine,
A tumbler of whiskey flows down my throat.
Another poem entered into the books,
Though be it
One that's lost it's rhyme.

(originally collected in 'Poet in the Long Dark Coat' - 2019)

The Day Will Come When The Light Subsides

The day will come when the light subsides
And unspent turmoil will leave an empty bay:
For even calm waters, they bare rough tides.

Behind the drapes hang her lies.
A gleaming smile but nout to say.
The day will come when the light subsides.

Innocence glitters within soft eyes,
Spite poisoned fang retracted ne'er displayed,
For even calm waters, they bare rough tides.

Framed portrait hung, bedside devotion amplified.
But pride of place too long soon paints their stabbing disdain.
The day will come when the light subsides.

Collected silence in time sees vengeful rise
As darkened clouds replace a summer's day,
For even calm waters they bare rough tides.

Failing love and a forgotten blindside,
Fool's hope drinks to groundhog day.
The day will come when the light subsides
For even calm waters, they bare rough tides.

(previously uncollected)

My Setting Sun

My heart a winter's woodland
Of barren soil and brush.
Snapped twigs under booted feet,
Love as slippery as the mudded, muddled,
Puddled ground.

Her heart, her soul, her memory,
The setting sun.
A brightening beauty, leaving
But still colouring my days.
Warm and blinding
And achingly out of reach.

And I trudge on
Through the long vacated trenches
Listening to tragic birdsong.
Leaning over the parapet to watch as she set,
Mourning the leaving love that I had always longed for.

(previously uncollected)

Flying My Wings

I live life in the fast lane.
That is to say, I learnt the art of not giving a fuck.
I say what I feel, think, and don't hide my mood.

I act upon impulses, and usually look the fool.
But at least at the end of it all
I can say I lived full.

I've been told
I'm intense
No pretence.
Mood swings,
But hey,
I'm just flying my wings.

I've made plenty of mistakes living this way
But on my last breath,
At least I won't be begging to stay.

(originally collected in 'The Random Ramblings of a Restless
Mind' - 2017)

Establishment

Stuck in this embryo
This confining seal.
Trapped in the system
Deadening.

I no longer feel.

Ordered here and there,
Do this and do that
Like some dog shit doormat.

There is no escape.
Young and vulnerable
Preyed on as the weak.
There is no escape.
dO thIs, dO thAt.
Work hard, skip meals.

Who's to say
How we should live our life?
We had it right
back in the 'era of love'.
Now, it's all wrong
In the era
of when push comes to shove.

(originally collected in 'Poetry in Motion' - 2013)

Society Needs A Saviour

Screaming cars
Disappearing stars.
Destructive youth
A saddening truth:
The world is becoming an ugly place,
And I
Am ashamed to show my face…

Kids without morals or manners
Dealing death like a game of cards.
Dagger scanners everywhere
Factions taking hold anywhere.
The world is becoming an ugly place,
And I
Am ashamed to show my face…

The chopping of trees
And polluting of seas
Total destruction of land
Humans
We are the damning damned.
Warming of the ice
Like a risky roll
of the dice.
As the fossil fuels
burnout,
Time is
Run-
-ning
out.

We all deserve a better world to live in.

The world is becoming an ugly place,
And I
Am ashamed to show my face…

Are you?

(originally collected in 'Poetry in Motion' - 2013)

Removing The Mask That Covers Us All

The moist soil of decades ago now sit beneath my feet of today.
I take my shoes off, the cold pierces the bottom of my feet.
The wet grass caressing and stroking
the nerve endings long numbed.

I kneel and place my palms down and feel nature herself.
Richmond Park,
Did Big H do this here too?

She is calm.
The wind shivers down my spine and brushes through my hair.

I look around to be sure that I am alone.
I am.
I take off the mask of society and roam free.

I am a satyr amongst the trees.
Shh.
I must not be found.

(originally collected in 'Poetry in Motion' - 2013)

I'm Hurt

I'm hurt.

I'm hurt because we are capable of having so much power as
a collective; but nobody is willing to look up from Facebook for
five minutes to see that actually,
we're all hurting.

We're all hurting together for different reasons; and yet for the
exact same reason.

I watch as people barge into each other without
even looking up from their phones and I think,
shit, that's me too!

I'm hurt.

I'm hurt because I look around me,
and I see

my generation.

And I wonder
are we going to be the ones that snap out of it and save the
world

or are we going to be so hooked to screens that'll we'll go
missing and be known as

the ones who could have but didn't.

(originally collected in 'The Random Ramblings of a Restless
Mind' - 2017)

Derelict Terrorist

You can try to beat us down
Little men with broken hearts
Broken minds
And tarnished souls.
You can try to destroy our way of life
By carrying out other's lies.
You can try to force on us your strife

But know this:

The people of London shall never fall.
We will continue to lead the world
Whilst united
And standing tall.

Two wrongs do not make a right.
Do not harm the people of the streets
For this is not
Their fight.

(originally collected in 'The Random Ramblings of a Restless
Mind' - 2017)

Land Of The Free

Guns pop off kids are screaming,
clothes are torn, a shoe is missing.
Lead and smoke fill the air,
a silence
lingers
eerily.
Teachers cower under desks,
alarms are ringing, children
trembling.
Bloodied homework
sweeps the floor.

A place of learning, suddenly burning.
Hell fire strikes,
the wall's a bullet furnace.

Senseless violence,
looped by minutes silence
a life lost before it's birth.
A pocketed dollar treasured over
an innocent life untouched.

They don't care.

So long as their bank accounts get filled
it doesn't matter who's blood is spilled.

And so the i n n o c e n t
are left to *grieve*,

And the high and ***mighty***
continue
to deceive.

(originally collected in 'Blue Streak' - 2018)

Poetic Quotes
Pt. II

And though my feet shiver in bitter cold,
drenched and squelching....
at least I walked through the flooded field.

(originally collected in 'The Random Ramblings of a Restless
Mind' - 2017)

Sleep... you are evasive once more.
But I do not weep, for I know that
I have the stars to keep me company this night.

(originally collected in 'The Random Ramblings of a Restless
Mind' - 2017)

What are you looking for?

Everything.

(originally collected in 'The Random Ramblings of a Restless
Mind' - 2017)

There's strength in simplicity.

(originally collected in 'Blue Streak' - 2018)

He wrote about the things most people neglected
For he mostly neglected people.

(originally collected in 'Blue Streak' - 2018)

Not every superhero wears a cape.
Some just have a bald head.

(originally collected in 'Blue Streak' - 2018)

You ARE enough.
You ARE beautiful.
You ARE gifted.
Your ARE inspiring.
You ARE loved.
You ARE needed.
Your ARE powerful.
You ARE everything!
I know because we all are
And that's what makes us uniquely great.

(originally collected in 'The Random Ramblings of a Restless Mind' - 2017)

AG

I'm stuck in a zoetrope.
Standing in the centre
as the world spins around me.
On the inside looking out,
my only glance of the world
through thin slits of tin.

(originally collected in 'Blue Streak' - 2018)

AG

To be a writer is to be in a constant state of vulnerability.
You have to be able to pick up inspiration the minute it hits. No matter where you are, who you're with or what you're doing.
It may be something as small as grass protruding through mud… you just HAVE to be susceptible.

(originally collected in 'Blue Streak' - 2018)

One day you'll look into a set of eyes,
and get so lost you won't ever find a way out,
but nor will you ever want to.

(originally collected in 'Blue Streak' - 2018)

Love can often be like flowers.
Sometimes they die, sometimes they don't.
Sometimes they grow back, sometimes they don't.
That's just the natural cycle
and we should take comfort in that.

(originally collected in 'Blue Streak' - 2018)

And her total desire for love
was the very reason she could not find it.

(originally collected in 'Blue Streak' - 2018)

Love has given me my greatest fear.
That one day I will fall asleep beside you
As 'your one true love',
and then wake up next to somebody totally and completely
new.
I fear that I may close my eyes and miss the moment
you suddenly fell out of love with me.
The moment I became a mere superfluous component.

(originally collected in 'Poet in the Long Dark Coat' - 2019)

AG

If only we were brave enough to
admit our burning desires
to one another.

(originally collected in 'The Random Ramblings of a Restless
Mind' - 2017)

You are always in control…
Of EVERYTHING.
No excuses.

(originally collected in 'Blue Streak' - 2018)

AG

Some call me weird.
I call it real.

(originally collected in 'Blue Streak' - 2018)

AG

My 'high bit S Drive'
Keeps getting me jammed.

(originally collected in 'Poet in the Long Dark Coat' - 2019)

My old wounds have become a part of who I am now.
My unseen scars
now cherished stars.

(originally collected in 'Poet in the Long Dark Coat' - 2019)

AG

She told everyone she was fine,
that she was happy.
But I could tell just by the way she slumped in her chair
she was a woman of falsehood.
That nobody had bothered to take care;
To listen to what she had truly said.
Too wrapped up in themselves I'd presume.

(originally collected in 'Poet in the Long Dark Coat' - 2019)

AG

I find windows the most amazing things.
The gateway into so many different hives.
I'm fascinated when I walk down the street and spot people
just going about their daily lives.

(originally collected in 'Blue Streak' - 2018)

I Hate Wine

Your shadow once covered the living room walls
As you stood looming tall
Bottle in hand
Before obliterating it
Onto the plaster and wooden floor.

My heart beat,
My mind swirled.
Brows furrowed,
Tongue curled.

Now I'm here
Standing in front
Of that same old wall
That same damn wall
Where you threw your wine
Your silhouette now mine
My body shaking in cold,
Sickened sweat.

Like father like son.
Fallen from the vine.
Thrown into the pit.

(previously uncollected)

The Ungiving Tree

A bird on each branch.
Eggs dropped
broken nests.
Your arms aren't made for homes
just plenty of thin leaves.
Just plenty
                    of leaves.

Oak tree replaced by Birch
We were supposed to be two
But a pairing cut down too soon
Fuel a fire
We weren't ever meant
            to be
                        close to   one another.

Winter.

                    Barren branches
                    Can't provide shade.
                Trees stand tall don't they?
                Unmoving and stubborn.

But summer will come again
The roots will keep me going
I won't die. I'll keep growing
As tall as you and maybe farther.

(previously uncollected)

Forgiven

Father don't cry.
Differences arise through time
But there won't ever be
A forever goodbye.
Maybe we didn't see eye to eye at the beginning,
Our relationship taking a hellova beating.
So we weren't close like the typical father and son,
But still somehow
We shared moments of blissful fun.
We were different. We were unique.
Don't worry, you did a good job despite your lack of
            technique.
We have moments that we hold dearly in our hearts
That will live on in memory until both us depart.

So don't worry. Don't be a fool.
You've given me a great start in this almighty whirlpool.

I'm not good at this with you,
Never was.
But I guess what I'm trying to say is,
Well,
You've done alright.

(originally collected in 'Poetry in Motion' - 2013)

Wake-Up

Drip drop dripping.
Early mornin' rain slipping.
Smiling and singing.
Singing and smiling.
Pitter patter patter pitter.
Beat beat beat.

Wakey wakey, rise and shine
"get your ass outta bed" she says.

But the moon his sun,
And the sun his moon.
Not even the pitter patter
drip drop dripping
singing
beat beat beating
rain
can wake him up.

(originally collected in 'The Random Ramblings of a Restless
Mind' - 2017)

A Poem for a Place I'd Rather Be

Ah, blissful night
Take me into your
beautiful blanket of serenity.
Lift me up now, oh won't you,
to the puffy clouds above.
Where I may slumber awhile,
away from the problematic chaos below.

Let the swirls of pinks and blues,
dotted with stars, swim in front of me
like ink and water collided in a
psychedelic aqua dance. Where the pan flutes
play as I lay,
cooled by vapoured chill.

Look at the glorious views! Just look!
Oh nothing can disturb my peace now.
No. Nothing.
As I slowly float adrift amongst the puffy
feathers.

And so take me down now, if you must,
but know that this is not the end. I may
wake and stir now, but I'll be back again
and return to your sweet touch.

(originally collected in 'The Random Ramblings of a Restless
Mind' - 2017)

Demons

He sat alone in the corner of his darkened room
Looking to his window.
The rain smashes upon the glass and frame
He's a courier of much emotion and pain.
Everyone he had ever known got up and left,
He lived then in complete unrest.
A new beginning, to start again.
The only friends he held were the local barmen.
The demons lingered inside him
Far superior than the voices of reason.
Life had been kind but he was blinded by ignorance.

Slowly they destroyed him, he could not find balance.

He got to his feet and ripped open his shirt
Baring his chest.
"Take me, I surrender,
Let me be at rest."

(originally collected in 'Poetry in Motion' - 2013)

It's Over

slowly
sinking
like the setting sun.
i'm sorry to say
but i'm officially
done.
it's time
to hangup
my mask.
time to find myself
a different task.
time to
drop
my pen.
on the paper
it lays
silent
and
still.
the dust
shall encase
my fingers
and emotion
as i seek solitude
in a secret
location.
failure,
that has
encompassed me
as success
finds
he.

of course pride and joy i send to him,
but what
motivates me
has worn
thin.

i have been entrapped
by the firm talons of the establishment.
and despite my
faux encouragement
and my gallivant efforts
i am
stuck
in a
routine.
mismanagement
of emotions.
pain.

my
world
has
crum-
-bled.

(originally collected in 'Poetry in Motion' - 2013)

Micro Poems
Pt. III

Darkest Depths

I can feel the inner demon
Rattling the cages within my soul.
"Feed me" it calls like a little Gremlin.

But I shall not give in to its falsely empowering ways.
He is the the shadow that walks beside me, behind me.
The darkest inhibitions.
A step ahead, or a step behind.

It is my duty to keep it
behind.

(originally collected in 'Poetry in Motion' - 2013)

The Worst Hurt

He broke her.
She made him and then without
his knowledge, he broke her.
Into a thousand shards
of brittle hurt.
Never knowing just how much.
She kept her mouth shut, weeping only after dark -
where no eyes would lurk to bear witness.
He hurt her and she took it to the grave with her.

(originally collected in 'The Random Ramblings of a Restless
Mind' - 2017)

Not The Man I'd Hoped To Me

And I've not become the man I'd hoped to be,
The love I sought has evaded me.
My dreams ran off away with me
And I'm beginning to accept,
Reality and mind may never meet.

Hooded eyes, bent spine,
Oily skin, and a voice that whines.
A darkened soul and wrinkled lines,
A pining mind;
A man no woman would seek to find.

And I've not become the man I'd hoped to be,
The love I sought has evaded me.
My dreams ran off away with me
And I'm beginning to accept,
Reality and mind may never meet.

(originally collected in 'Poet in the Long Dark Coat' - 2019)

Innocence

The child in me has all but left my side.
Except that one part,
That even now
To think of makes me smile.

My innocence was stripped.
My naivety taught.
My adventures were somehow lost
And my jokes, they only got worse.

But the capacity to love
And be loved
And seek LOVE,

That I cannot seem to shake.

(previously uncollected)

Spontaneous Prose

Fee fop fadoodle,
where the fucks my poodle?!

Oh wait, I don't have one.

Half awake, half dead to the world.
Spontaneous prose, what a kick!

(originally collected in 'The Random Ramblings of a Restless
Mind' - 2017)

Lumpy Dump Gov.

I'm stumped.
The government keeps taking a lumpy dump,
Right on my head; down every avenue I tread.
Thank you Mrs. May.

And there were days when Trump was something that came
Out of my arse,
Imagine that. But now,
Now it's a man in power,
Sitting in front of the big red button.
My throat tightens with a lump.
What a c...

(originally collected in 'Poet in the Long Dark Coat' - 2019)

Daylight Savings

Hey you!
Daylight thieves!
Stop charging me double for half the
produce, damn it!
That's daylight robbery!
70 pence for a chocolate the size
of my pinky?! That's stinky! You're not
suffering, still making millions,
whilst I scrimp and scrape for my favourite biscuit.

(originally collected in 'The Random Ramblings of a Restless
Mind' - 2017)

Time

Time is a murderous unseen thief named Emit.
A running snowball down a summer's hill.
Lost in the tick tock, tick tock
In everything we'd wished not
Sitting in a corner timid
We wasted away hoping things would just stand still.

(previously uncollected)

Botched Law

A man walked out in front of my car today
He thought it was worth a laugh.
And for a second, my mind chose not to find
The all too present break pedal.
Natural selection should be exempt from the law.

(previously uncollected)

Sticks and Stones

I was not born into wealth and privilege.
Instead I was made to carve from a single stone
A life that just about got me by.
Scrimping and scraping, breaking bones.
Sitting on a throne
Erected from love and trust,
I build my foundation
From feebly thrown sticks and stones.

(previously uncollected)

Just for Us

There are stars that shine so bright.
But they are not the ones that interest me.
No.
The ones that interest me are the dimly lit ones.
The ones that despite being pushed furthest away,
Are still working their hardest to be up there
In the night sky
Just for us.

(previously uncollected)

The Warmest Glow

The warmest glow
Is a solidary candle
Burning in the dead of night.
Calming in the darkness
Setting the world to rights.

(previously uncollected)

Too Much To Ask

All he asked
Was she see his smile.
Return his hugs.
To hold his hand.

To understand his pain.

And in return,
He would give her the world.

(previously uncollected)

Forbidden Fruit

How do I tell you I want you,
when I know you're forbidden fruit.
Don't go acting coy though, cos I know
you want me too.

(originally collected in 'The Random Ramblings of a Restless
Mind' - 2017)

Do Not Weep

Do not weep at our departure.
You shall think of me again one day,
and you can be sure that I'll be thinking of you.
And so with that in mind, it shall be like we are
together once more.

Though distanced in reality by land miles wide,
I shall meet you in your thoughts
and be standing by your side.

(originally collected in 'The Random Ramblings of a Restless
Mind' - 2017)

Squeetious*

Oh, just feel how soft her hand sits upon my chest
How gentle it slides, into a sweet and loving caress
Isn't she so lovely!? So squeetiously* cuddly!
She's my English rose, my inspired prose!
She's the breath in my lungs,
The heroin unsung.

(originally collected in 'Poet in the Long Dark Coat' - 2019)

———————

*   See index on page 108.

Moon's Star

And I know that no matter how far we part
If we both stop and stare at the moon
Wherever we are
We're standing together
Another of the moon's stars.

(originally collected in 'Blue Streak' - 2018)

Will You?

Sitting here thinking of you
missing you
wanting you.

But none of that makes
any difference because
you'll never know,
will you?

(originally collected in 'The Random Ramblings of a Restless
-2017')

B.S Bitch

You came to me,
and I thought you shined like a diamond.
But I was mistaken.
What really shone was the edge of your knife,
as it caught the light's reflection.

(originally collected in 'Blue Streak' - 2018)

Words for my Grave

And if you're reading these words
It means I've met my death.
So here lay my bones,
My lungs short of breath.
My heart no longer beats
And my mind,
It finally rests.

Adam Richard Charles Gary
05/05/92 -

(previously uncollected)

SIMPLEX METRES

Simplex Metre 1

Crying.
Sadness.
He left.

An explanation on Simplex Metres: Simplex Metre. I have been playing around a lot recently with my poetry, trying to expand from the usual rhymes, and typical metres. I have been reading a lot of Jack Kerouac and Charles Bukowski, as well as looking at Kerouac's 'Spontaneous Prose' and the traditional Japanese Haiku Poems.

This lead me to start wondering, could I create my own form of poetry? I started thinking about what made the 21st century unique. The three words that came to mind were: Simplicity, Convenience, Lazy.

So with these words in mind, and the influence of Spontaneous Prose, and Haikus I went to work; and so was born the 'Simplex Metre'. Three lines, two syllables each, made from lines of one word, one word, two words.

Creating a poem that stirs imagery and emotion using this form takes some creative thinking, and whether it works or not I'm not sure.

Simplex Metre 2

Doorway.
Opportunes
Blocked Closed.

Simplex Metre 3

Running.
Escape.
He's Hurt.

Simplex Metre 4

Madness
Clutching
His Mind.

Simplex Metre 4

Madness
Clutching
His Mind.

Simplex Metre 5

Simple.
Forever.
Good Life.

Simplex Metre 6

Forgive.
Forget.
Have Faith.

Simplex Metre 7

Loving,
Laughing,
Fun times.

Simplex Metre 8

Darkness.
Laptop.
Sweet bliss.

Simplex Metre 9

Sunshine
radiates.
Smiles wide.

Simplex Metre 10

Entrapped.
Helpless.
He lost.

Simplex Metre 11

Darkness
Alone
Nothing

Simplex Metre 12

Boiling
Anger
Clenched Fist

Simplex Metre 13

Swelling
Sockets
The hurt

Simplex Metre 14

Burning
Headache
His loss

Swirls of the Neurotic Flames

Swirls of the neurotic flames
A depressing truth that there's

                                                nothing left to gain.
No future here
                Nothing but
uselessness
                  and corrupted arrogance.
Nothing that   endures us
only   '
        The Fear.'

In a world that's doomed
One must continue to struggle to find the ever escaping light.

Within the flames I may lose myself from time to time,
But freedom   within insanity is a beautiful thing.

(originally collected in 'Poetry in Motion' - 2013)

Insecurity

The weakling that is inside of me.
The demon that encompasses me.

The materialisation of my insecurity.

Frail like a brittle stick,
A man should be a brick,
You dick!

I can't cope with it...
All this negative shit.

                    I feel physically sick.
            It's like a crowbar wrenching out my intestines.

I hang my head and
Stare at the ground,
Here we go again
I'm depression bound,
But don't worry
I'm used to it.

(originally collected in 'Poetry in Motion' - 2013)

I Want To Feel

i feel dead inside, emotionless.
i feel like the world could crumble beneath me
and i wouldn't even feel a thing.

i want to feel happy,
i want to feel strong.
i want to feel something.
i want to feel alive again.

i want to chase the end of the rainbow to find the pot of gold.

I want to be rescued.

(originally collected in 'Poetry in Motion' - 2013)

Happy New Year

we stood on either side of the room at the new years party
our eyes locked as you sipped your glass of wine
and i was reminded of the nights we spent
emptying a bottle and playing card of humanity,
mocking humanity.

and then your eyes met the ground
mine still locked on you
and i saw like me our times are yet to be forgotten.

i wish i had never told you anything.
i wish i had never uttered the words of how you made me feel
that night.
i wish that i could have gone on pretending like life was just a
dream.
a dream where i could lay in your arms locked away
never disturbed.
but you held my cheek that night
red wine blanketing your lips
and you told me how different a dream it was for you.
and in three words you bulldozed everything i had struggled
to build
as you whispered through ever blushing cheeks
angelic cruelty
"I'm so sorry."

(previously uncollected)

A Lesson atop Tywardreath Hills

The summer sunset sinks beneath the hills
The trickling sound of Jack Daniels poured.
The smell of sizzling beef laid out upon the grill
As we sit here in Tywardreath abroad.

Watching the sky's golden glow
As the world out there passes slow
My uncle steps up and with a chink of our glasses,
Our preferred poison,
He tells me there's something he wants me to know.

And he squeezes my shoulder with great affection
As we stare out at the setting sun
The warm summer's evening a beautiful distraction.

And he says
In life you need to learn to be as hard as rubber
Soft as nails.
Live life slowly like the hares
And as fast as snails.
Be tough like a sensual caress
But soft like the slugger.
Be a gentleman, but also a bugger.
Take your time but don't waste your time.
Lessons and words for you to live by boy
If you're to find in this life any true joy.

And he looks at me before laughing
Winking at me like a man gone batty
Before flipping the fatty beef burger patties.

(originally collected in 'Poet in the Long Dark Coat' - 2019)

Daisie

And how I wish I'd spelt her name Daisie.
For she had a soul that was far more worthy
Than the
singular
Daisy.
Singularity
Disgracefully
Inadequate.

Daisy,
Your small beating heart gave more
Than I had ever anticipated
The day we met.
And how I remember that morn' indeed.
Sat pressed against the glass
With nothing to say
At Dog's Trust, Harefield
Your back turned to us
Wondering how you'd gotten to be there.
And you craned your neck quietly
Collectedly amongst the chaos
Happy even then to see our unknown faces.
You licked us through the holes softly like you hadn't a hope
in the world.

And there's no feeling
Like when I carried you in my arms
My little loving pooch.
Who will save me now you're gone,
Who can do what you had done?

And though your journey may not have started with us
I can only hope now that it has come to an end
You are as thankful to have found us
As we are to have found you.

(previously uncollected)

Daisy

There wasn't a star in sight
That night I received the news.
Dull were my views,
Bleak and grey
The expected truth.
My world
       fell apart.
Other's words of comfort
Keeping her together on my behalf.

Her eyes, innocence, and purest heart
Captured forever in a tribute photograph.
She was my companion
Loyal and full of compassion
Me a poor Aramis, her... a far better
D'Artagnan

(originally collected in 'Poet in the Long Dark Coat' - 2019)

Poetic Quotes
Pt. III

He smiled
she smiled.
She smiled
they smiled.

I've travelled distances on this earth
but nowhere near as far as that smile.
So smile.

(originally collected in 'Blue Streak' - 2018)

AG

If we don't learn to sit with the dark,
how can we possibly appreciate the importance of
light?

(originally collected in 'Blue Streak' - 2018)

AG

I've literally got to be the
luckiest guy in the world.
The things my eyes manage to capture
in this lifetime are just beyond words.
How did I get so lucky?

(originally collected in 'Blue Streak' - 2018)

we seem to have found ourselves in a period of time where innocent until proven guilty doesn't mean a thing.

a man's life can be ruined by rumour, a woman shunned by wrongful slander. and even a world at war from accusations backed by no evidence.

centuries of work pissed up the wall.

(originally collected in 'Blue Streak' - 2018)

Have you ever observed a field for a lengthy amount
of time? One minute they're constantly being cut
short, trimmed, controlled… but then one day they're
left alone, and they grow so tall you can become
tangled in the grass. Keep persevering, one day your
moment will come and nobody will hold you back.

(originally collected in 'Blue Streak' - 2018)

A single blade of grass
Is nothing to consider special.
But accompanied by a hundred or more by it's side
creates a beautiful field to be admired.

(originally collected in 'Poet in the Long Dark Coat' - 2019)

There will be times when you feel sad.
Like, really sad.
And it'll hurt too.
Trust me, I know.
But make an effort to remind yourself that
life is always evolving, revolving, and resolving.

(originally collected in 'Poet in the Long Dark Coat' - 2019)

Women are a magical breed.
You immediately know when there is a significant
female in your life, because they bring a
particular warmth. A fuzzing glow.
Suddenly a weight is lifted from your shoulder
and everything feels alright.

(originally collected in 'The Random Ramblings of a Restless
Mind' - 2017)

I don't bed the woman,
she beds me.
I can't pull off those lines of sleaze
and they're really into poetry.

(originally collected in 'The Random Ramblings of a Restless
Mind' - 2017)

One minute we were just friends fooling around,
The next I'm on my knees, falling down,
Tongue out totally in love.
(originally collected in 'Poet in the Long Dark Coat' - 2019)

I was always going to crash and burn.
It was only a question
Of when and how.

(originally collected in 'Poet in the Long Dark Coat' - 2019)

Scarlette

She Came To Me As Waves Do The Shore

Her eyes look left and right but never straight
Constellations that shine soft yet always bright.
Gentle spoken poems from tendered page
A grace she holds beyond the words she types.
She came to me as waves do the shore
For kindred hearts seek single boats at sea.
Nature plucked her strings and played her score
As two poets danced to cupid's spree.
Though distanced are we by global pandemic
Dates confined to DMs and a Netflix movie,
So soon I'll set sail across the Atlantic
To gaze upon the face of true beauty.
She came to me as waves do the shore
And now she'll stay in memory evermore.

(previously uncollected)

Coming Home[*]

We boarded the same train
Didn't know where to
But now I know I'm coming home
Coming home to you

Seats don't come cheap these days
And they said mind the gap or we'd fall.
On these rails of steel
The whole world seems so small
Doesn't matter how we're parted
Half the fun is in the view
But always coming back to where we started
When I'm coming home
Coming home to you

Dated tickets ablaze passing by the window
Old flames burn dull
Paper cut hearts left to ash on the platform
But we'll be stronger than we were before
Sparks fly under our feet
Taking our time so we last forever
Stay in the sleeping car tonight
Home is good but the journey is better

The tracks can get tough
But we always pull through
Because I know I'm coming home
Coming home to you

(previously uncollected)
*2 see index on page 108

Scarlette II

A Thousand Miles and More

A thousand miles and more away she waits,
Sorrowed calls as the saddened owl at night.
A thousand miles and more away he aches,
Heart bursting through a nightmare lullaby.
Our lines steel strings plucked straight from the heart
As each new verse, we further to heaven.
Stubborn land and sea do keep us apart
But rest, my soul resides now in Princeton.
Stanza'd bridge and fragranced envelopes
Can't mask our thirst of touch like the Pansies to Ether's eye.
Our hearts jailed in a dingy cell alone
Bail set at an astronomical high.
If I could hold you for just a deep breath
I'd drop it all and…

(previously uncollected)

And In Our Loneliness We Came Together

An Early Corona Poem on Unrealised Hope

Can a summer's day be the same
Enjoyed only through a sterile windowpane?
Is a lover's smile still warming
When it's from 5 or 6 feet away?
Is the sky still blue, and the sun still warm?
The Sparrow's song
Still a melodic call?

Empty streets, nature plays.
Silent blanket, longer days.
Books now read, films a plenty,
Board games, laughter, frowns are many -
Family bonds once lost regained.

Mother Earth's beautiful web re-spinning
As numbers and timetables couldn't keep us stable.
Clamped to a lonely household, our jumper cable
A return to life by beating heart, threatens a new beginning.

And in our loneliness we came together.
In seperation we bonded.
Beyond the keys and beyond the screens
We were saved by our humanity.
So water the flowers,
Feel the breeze through an opened window.
Cherish all day's hour,
And listen for the Lark's call.
For in years to come we'll hear them say
Isolation wasn't a loss, but an opportunity that was gained.

(previously uncollected)

The Early Hours

Let not the leaves of first summer
fall in vain.
Let not the bud's beauty wilt before its
blooming spectacle.
Let not blue skies juvenile
cloud over before an august reign
Nor burn too soon the work of
lame Hephaestus.

Unexceptional anvilled chassis
The basis of Apollo's pruning.
Chiron on the winding road
Leading through the gated abbey.

And now the winter turns to spring
Seeds become our stalks.
Dion sleeps on a bed of stone
Draped in petals freshly plucked.
Noon has risen to shine her beauty
and bid adieu
to the morning dew.
Her loving rays give birth
And warms away the fresh and welcoming
of these early hours.

(previously uncollected)

Don't mind me, I was just randomly rambling from a restless mind…

Index

With Thanks

With thanks to everyone who has supported me on this journey so far. You all know who you are. We're just getting started...

Lightning Source UK Ltd.
Milton Keynes UK
UKHW040059090223
416676UK00005BA/335